Prime Time 8

Speaking

Georg Hellmayr

Stephan Waba

www.oebv.at

Table of contents

You will need internet access to complete this task.

PTT 5 = Prime Time 5 Transition (ISBN 978-3-209-08063-9 | SBNR 165463)
PT 5 = Prime Time 5 (ISBN 978-3-209-06705-0 | SBNR 150124)
PT 6 = Prime Time 6 (ISBN 978-3-209-07159-0 | SBNR 155137)
PT 7 = Prime Time 7 (ISBN 978-3-209-07160-6 | SBNR 155138)
PT 8 = Prime Time 8 (ISBN 978-3-209-07161-3 | SBNR 160179)

Einleitung

Die kompetenzorientierte Reifeprüfung überprüft sprachliche Fertigkeiten, die von den Schülerinnen und Schülern beherrscht werden müssen. An Allgemeinbildenden Höheren Schulen ist das Niveau B2 des Gemeinsamen Europäischen Referenzrahmens für Sprachen (GERS) zu erreichen.

Der mündliche Teil der kompetenzorientierten Reifeprüfung besteht aus zwei Aufgabenbereichen zum selben Thema:

- **Individual long turn:** Bei dieser **monologischen Aufgabe** muss die Fragestellung ausgehend von zwei Bildern, die einander gegenübergestellt werden, behandelt werden. Für diese Aufgabenstellung steht ein Zeitraum von etwa fünf Minuten zur Verfügung.

- **Paired activity:** Im Bereich der **dialogischen Aufgabe** diskutieren zwei Personen (Schüler/in – Schüler/-in bzw. Schüler/in – Lehrer/in) einen Sachverhalt nach speziellen Vorgaben. Für diesen Bereich sind etwa zehn Minuten vorgesehen.

Die detaillierten Bestimmungen sind der Reifeprüfungsverordnung (BGBl. II – Ausgegeben am 30. Mai 2012 – Nr. 174) zu entnehmen.

Der vorliegende Band bereitet auf die Prüfungsformate und Themenbereiche vor, die bei der kompetenzorientierten Reifeprüfung im Bereich Sprechen zu erwarten sind. Jedem der vorgegebenen Themenbereiche wurde ein Abschnitt gewidmet.

Jeder Abschnitt bietet auf einer Doppelseite realistische *speaking prompts* (monologisch und dialogisch) zum jeweiligen Thema sowie Übungsmöglichkeiten und Wortschatzübersichten sowohl zu den Themen selbst als auch zu typischen sprachlichen Funktionen. Gerade das direkte Ansteuern von kommunikativen Funktionen (z. B. Zustimmung und Ablehnung) wird mit diesen Bereichen erleichtert und gefestigt. Damit kann auch unabhängig vom jeweiligen Thema der Wortschatz erweitert und die Ausdrucksfähigkeit gesteigert werden.

Eine Übersicht über sämtliche Kapitel der Lehrwerksreihe von der 5. bis zur 8. Klasse, die den Vorgaben entsprechend den 24 Themenkreisen des Themenpools zugeordnet sind, ergänzt den Übungsteil.

Wo es möglich ist, bietet dieser Band die Lösungen zu den Aufgabenstellungen (s. S. 64).

Anleitungen und Tipps, wie diese Aufgaben gut zu bewältigen sind, finden sich auch in den Anhängen des Lehrwerks *Prime Time* der Klassen 5 bis 8 *(skills pages, spot on language, exam preparation guide)*. Es empfiehlt sich, diese Abschnitte immer wieder zur Wiederholung und Festigung der nötigen Fertigkeiten heranzuziehen.

Der Bereich Sprechen erfordert besonders viel Übung und darüber hinaus die genaue Kenntnis der Prüfungsmodalitäten. Mit den Materialien aus diesem Band können diese Fertigkeiten intensiv geübt werden. Sie bieten eine Grundlage, um eine erfolgreiche Reifeprüfung zu gewährleisten.

Das Autorenteam wünscht Ihnen dabei guten Erfolg!

Topic 1 Relationships and social networks

Tasks

1 Individual long turn: Having a child

- *Compare and contrast the two pictures.*
- *Discuss how having a child may influence a couple's life.*
- *Explain the challenges the two couples might have to face.*

2 Paired activity: Organising the perfect date

You and your partner have a common friend who is very shy and has problems meeting new people. You know that he/she fancies a boy/girl from your school. In order to help him/her to meet this boy/girl, you decide to organise the perfect date for your friend.

Discuss the following aspects:

- *location*
- *time*
- *food*
- *music*
- *other participants*

Decide which points are essential for the success of the date. Agree on three.

Support material: Describing a picture

1 Giving the main facts

If you want to describe a picture, it is a good idea to start your description with the sentence: "This is a picture of ... ."

Look at each picture carefully and answer these questions:
- Where do you think this is?
- Who do you think the people are?
- What are the people doing?

> The picture was taken in/at/near ... . • The photo was taken in/at/during ... . •
> The picture depicts/shows ... .

2 Getting the words right

Start by collecting a number of useful words that relate to the pictures.

> bottle • boy • can • child • cooler bag • country house • to cuddle • dog •
> to embrace • father • girl • grass • to laugh • lunchbox • mother • picnic blanket •
> to play with • porch • sandwich • to smile • sofa • wood • young

3 Adding adjectives

Adjectives are words that describe nouns, for example: a **happy** boy, a **relaxed** mother, a **sunny** day, ...
When you describe a picture, you can use adjectives to make your description more interesting. You can talk about how many people are in the picture, what clothes they are wearing and how they are feeling.

> adorable • agreeable • angry • beautiful • bewildered • brave • calm • cheerful •
> clumsy • eager • elderly • elegant • embarrassed • faithful • fancy • fierce • gentle •
> glamorous • grumpy • handsome • happy • helpless • ill • intelligent • jealous •
> jolly • kind • lazy • lively • mischievous • miserable • mysterious • nervous • nice •
> obedient • obnoxious • old-fashioned • optimistic • panicky • pessimistic • practical •
> proud • rebellious • relieved • scary • self-assured • shy • silly • strict • strong •
> thoughtless • well-built • witty • worried • young

4 Providing details

Finally, provide details on what the people are doing and where they are.

> at the bottom • at the top • behind • in front of • in the background • in the central part •
> in the foreground • in the lower part • in the middle • in the upper part • near • next to •
> on the left • on the left-hand side • on the right • on the right-hand side

Speculate about possible reasons for their behaviour and about possible consequences of what they are doing.

> The characters look as if ... . • The picture inspires the viewer to think about ... . •
> The picture makes the viewer feel ... . • The viewer has the impression that ... .

Topic 2 Home and surroundings

Tasks

1 **Individual long turn: Future homes**

- *Compare and contrast the two pictures.*
- *Evaluate the living conditions in these surroundings.*
- *Speculate about housing trends in the future.*

2 Paired activity: Neighbourhood watch

In your area, a group of citizens wants to introduce a neighbourhood watch scheme, forcing everybody in the area to watch out for potential criminals. You and your partner are not sure if you'd like to participate or not.

Discuss the following aspects:

- *change in lifestyle*
- *cooperation with the police*
- *consequences for young people*
- *general attitude towards others*
- *other options*

Decide whether such a move would make sense for you or not.

Support material: Explaining

1 Housing and surroundings

Types of houses	Buying and selling	Features of a property
terraced house	to market a property	Victorian front
bungalow	to make a profit	layout of the house/flat
semi-detached house	to consider an offer	small bathroom
town house	good profit margin	plumbing
mansion	to have to change features	kitchen fittings
skyscraper	can be fixed	beautiful features
flat	estate agent	timber features
basement flat	to purchase a house	traditional features
block of flats	asking price	garden
high-rise building	property market	front/back garden
penthouse	mortgage	terrace
cottage	to stay on budget	conservatory
farm house	to accept an offer	garden shed

Describing where properties are located		
residential area	neighbourhood	market town
nice area	village	country town
urban area	town	countryside
rural area	city	in the country
industrial area	suburb	on the coast

Housing development		
prices rise/go up	people move out of the city	people make a profit
prices fall	people move to the countryside	people look for a good profit
people sell	people can afford sth./to live in	
people buy/purchase	people lose money	

2 Phrase builder: Explaining

a) Combine the phrases on housing with phrases that are often used to explain and form meaningful sentences.

b) Write down at least ten of these sentences and memorise them.

The reason for … .	It was like this: … .	It's like this: … .
This is all due/down to … .	… is caused by … .	All stems from … .
… can be attributed to … .	We can put it all down to … .	Why is it that … ?
… is connected with … .	That is exactly why … .	That is why … .
It has turned out that … .	It emerged that … .	The trouble is that … .
The thing is that … .	There is only one explanation for … .	This leads to … .

Example:

The reason for people to move out of cities is that house prices have gone up enormously over the last few years.

Topic 3   Fashion and trends

Tasks

1 **Individual long turn: The way we dress**

- *Compare and contrast the two pictures.*
- *Describe how fashion influences the impression people make on us.*
- *Discuss your own favourite fashion style.*

2 **Paired activity: Time for a change**

You and your partner want to change your style(s) and your looks completely in order to be successful in a job interview. You are not sure what to do and go through a number of options together.

Discuss the following aspects:

- *types of clothes*
- *colours*
- *hairstyle*
- *make-up*
- *body modifications (e.g. tattoos, piercings)*

Decide which changes might be most promising for the job interview. Agree on three.

Support material: Comparing and contrasting

1 General phrases

This is very different from what I expected. • If you compare … to/with … . •
… has often been compared to/with … . • In contrast to/with … . •
There's no comparison between their … . • There the likeness ends. •
The two are quite alike, but … . • What differentiates her from … .

2 Sentence builders

… is	exactly precisely just virtually practically more or less almost nearly approximately about	the same as … .

… is	considerably a great deal (very) much (quite) a lot rather somewhat a little slightly hardly only a little	smaller bigger cheaper …	than … .

3 Comparing and contrasting

More than	On the same level as	Less/Fewer than

considerably better than
far superior to
(very) much better than
	to work in the same way as
	to be similar to
	to be like sth. else
	to be of equal value
	no difference between
	The same is true of … .
	It works out about the same,
	    whether … .
	It always adds up to the same
	    thing.
		less and less
		far less interesting than
		much worse than
		does not bear comparison with
		fewer items than

Topic 4 Nutrition, health and welfare

Tasks

1 Individual long turn: We are what we eat

- *Compare and contrast the two pictures.*
- *Discuss how our attitude to food has changed over the last few decades.*
- *Recommend how people should deal with food in the future.*

2 Paired activity: Healthy lifestyle for adults

Apart from food, there are a lot of other aspects that contribute to a healthy lifestyle. In your school, your class has started a project on healthy living to combat long-term effects. You and your partner take part and are responsible for advice and recommendations to adults, especially your teachers and parents.

Discuss the following aspects:

- *description of the present situation*
- *physical and mental activities*
- *job-related challenges*
- *stress management*
- *role models*

Decide what kind of advice you would give.

Support material: Expressing likes and dislikes

1 Talking about health issues

a) Go on the internet and search using the following keywords:
- food + healthy + future
- "How to deal with stress"

b) Read at least two of the texts that come up and make a list of five useful phrases/expressions you would like to remember.

2 Expressing likes and dislikes

a) Take items of food, people and activities and form sentences with the phrases from the table below.
b) Write down at least five phrases for each category to memorise.

	Likes	Dislikes
Food	to find sth. enjoyable to like sth. to love sth. to have a soft spot for sth. to be crazy about sth. to have a passion for sth.	to hate sth. to be not able to stand sth. to not like sth. … does not agree with me. Usually I don't eat … .
People	to appreciate sb. to like sb. to love sb. to admire sb. to be fond of sb. to adore sb. to think well of sb. to be attached to sb. to respect sb. to fancy sb. to be mad about sb. to find sb. attractive to have a crush on sb. What I really/most like about … is … .	to hate sb. to be not able to stand sb. to not like sb. to detest sb. to loathe sb. to find sb. appalling/impossible to find sb. unable to bear to be not able to bear sb. to detest sb. to despise sb. The worst thing is that … . What I really hate is the way … .
Activities	to be fond of doing sth. to like doing sth. to enjoy doing sth. to quite enjoy doing sth. to find/take pleasure in doing sth. to be into doing sth. to be keen on doing sth. to do sth. for fun	to dislike sth. to find sth. intolerable to hate sth. to not like sth. to loathe sth. Such behaviour is totally unacceptable.

3 How to start a sentence

Look at the sentence starters below and underline the ones that do not indicate a clear opinion.

I am not in a position to comment on … . • I am not in a position to judge … . •
I don't think that … . • My feeling is that … . • I don't want to comment on … . •
Well, actually, … . • I find it hard to … . • I personally … . • I really think that … . •
I would rather not comment on … . • I've honestly never thought about … . • If you ask me, … . •
In my opinion, … . • It depends on what you mean by … . • It is hard to say … . •
It's really quite simple … . • Look at it this way … .

Topic 5 Sports

Tasks

1 **Individual long turn: What is sport?**

- *Compare and contrast the two pictures.*
- *Describe which features make the two activities shown a sport and which don't.*
- *Discuss your personal attitude towards sports.*

2 **Paired activity: The ideal sports class for us**

Your class is going to Britain to attend an English course. In the information material that you received to prepare for the trip, the organisers ask you to choose one sports class as a daily afternoon programme. There are six different sports on offer: cycling, horse riding, tennis, climbing, swimming and beach volleyball. You are not sure which sport suits your class best and so you go through a number of options.

Discuss the following aspects:

- *level of fitness needed*
- *level of expertise needed*
- *equipment*
- *fun factor*
- *dangers*

Decide which sports class is the ideal one for your class.

Support material: Agreeing and supporting

1 Agreeing

But of course! • I (totally) agree with you. • I agree with what you say. • I couldn't agree more. •
I know exactly what you mean. • I quite/totally/absolutely agree. • I suppose that's generally true. •
I think that's rather/pretty good. • I think you are absolutely right. • Neither/Nor do I. • So do I. •
That's a great idea! • That's a(n) excellent/great/good idea. • That's what I think! •
That's a good point. • What a good idea. • Yes, I'm all for it/… . • You are absolutely right.

2 Agreeing in part

I see what you mean, I'd go along with you on that up to a point, That's a valid point, They have got a case, You could be right, You may be right there, You've got a point,	but yet however	I don't think it would work. the costs are very high. it's not the whole story. I'm not convinced. others might not agree.

3 Showing approval

More informally	More formally
I think that is a good idea. • I think that is a good suggestion/strategy/plan. • You are right to … . • We agree with your decision not to … . • I (really) liked the way … . • I was really impressed by … .	We are in broad agreement with … . • He/She (quite) rightly emphasises … . • One can only admire … . • We are very/enormously impressed with … . • We welcome … . • We are delighted with … . • I would like to express my complete support for … . • It is easy to understand how … . • The best solution would certainly be … . • One has only to glance at these lines … . • It was high time that … .

4 Supporting an argument

In a discussion it is sometimes necessary to support your argument with a statement an expert has made:

- A and B argue that … .
- As C, Associate Professor of Chemistry, notes … .
- Journalist D offers another perspective: … .

to accept • to acknowledge • to add (to) • to admit • to agree (to) • to argue • to believe •
to claim • to confirm • to declare • to defend • to demonstrate • to deny •
to dispute • to emphasise • to explore • to illustrate • to imply • to insist (on) • to justify •
to note • to observe • to point out • to recognise • to reject • to state • to suggest •
to think • to write

Topic 6 School and education

Tasks

1 Individual long turn: Learning styles

- *Compare and contrast the two pictures.*
- *Comment on the learning styles shown in the pictures.*
- *Describe your own preferred learning style and its effect on your performance.*

2 Paired activity: How to learn in the future

The publisher of a magazine on education has asked you and your partner to make suggestions for a learning environment for the future. You brainstorm ideas together.

Discuss the following aspects:

- *shortcomings of present systems*
- *technical requirements*
- *activities of the students*
- *interaction between students and teachers*
- *examinations*

Decide which aspects are the most important ones. Agree on three.

Support material: Disagreeing and rejecting

1 **Disagreeing and rejecting**

Read the following statements and disagree. Use the phrases provided to complete the statements and add a reason for your rejection.

1. Learning in groups doesn't lead anywhere. It is so distracting to work with others.

   I just don't accept that

2. You should focus more on your assignments. Don't just spend time with your friends.

   I'm afraid I couldn't possibly

3. Computers should not be used in class. Working with them is just a waste of time.

   I completely/totally disagree with that.

4. Currently, our technical equipment is not good enough to do e-learning.

   I don't think that's quite right.

5. Many older people are afraid of using modern technology in everyday life.

   That's not how I see it.

2 **Statements on education and schooling**

Combine the phrases to produce meaningful statements about education. Write down as many statements as possible.

Working independently	helps to focus on	young learners.
Working together with others in a group	raises the motivation of	students.
Noise in class	is/are more entertaining for	everybody.
Not using German in your English lesson	is a real challenge for	weaker learners.
Computer-generated exercises	is inspiring for	your tasks.
Listening to others	takes a lot of discipline	talented students.
Everybody in a group	is a major problem for	each other.
Agreeing with others in a team	can learn from	on all sides.

Example:

Working independently is a real challenge for young learners.

Topic 7   The world of work

Tasks

1 **Individual long turn: Different workplaces**

- *Compare and contrast the two pictures.*
- *Discuss which qualities and talents are needed to work in the jobs shown.*
- *Describe which workplace best suits your personal preferences.*

2 **Paired activity: Getting a holiday job**

You and your partner are planning to get a holiday job in the summer to earn some money. There are various jobs on offer: camp counsellor in a holiday camp for teenagers, cashier in a supermarket, cashier in a fast food restaurant, office assistant, factory worker at an assembly line and lab assistant in a research laboratory. You are not sure which job to apply for and so you talk about a number of options.

Discuss the following aspects:

- *workplace*
- *level of knowledge/expertise needed*
- *money*
- *working hours*
- *personal interest*

Decide which job is the ideal one for both of you.

Support material: Linking ideas

1 Linking words and phrases

Linking words/phrases show relationships between ideas or arguments. They are used to join two or more sentences or clauses. Linking words/phrases can be used to add ideas, contrast them or show the reason(s) for something.

2 Adding ideas and information

also	I want to be an astronaut. I **also** want to be a biologist. What should I do?
as well as	I checked various online job offers today. **As well as** that, I brushed up my CV.
besides	I can't afford to go to work by car every day. **Besides**, I don't really like driving.
for instance/ for example	**For instance**, focusing on the unemployment rate has its drawbacks.
in addition	**In addition**, jobs in environmental science are expected to grow by 25 per cent in the next two years.
moreover	**Moreover**, we know that these products can be globally successful.

3 Showing reasons

as/ since	**As** the deadline for job applications has already passed, we are unable to accept you.
because	Vocational training is growing quickly **because** employment pressures mean that people are spending more money and time on learning new skills.

4 Showing results

as a consequence/ consequently	This is the fourth time that this has happened and, **as a consequence**, we can't accept further services from you.
as a result	He's had six different jobs and, **as a result**, hasn't been moving up the career ladder.
so	**So** most of them had to close down.

5 Contrasting ideas

although/ though	**Although** many of us are quick to complain about our hours at work, the working week adds a certain stability and structure to our lives.
but	Well, I don't think of it as work. It *is*, **but** it's also fun.
despite/ in spite of	**Despite** the practical and emotional challenges of the job, there are tens of thousands of really fantastic care workers.
however	**However**, forcing hospitals to lay people off is not a good strategy for improving overall public health.
nevertheless	**Nevertheless**, online recruitment in the sector has significantly risen.
whereas/ while	Young graduates are chasing for the few jobs on offer **whereas** the majority are not qualified to pick up those jobs because of their inexperience.

Topic 8   Hobbies and spare time activities

Tasks

1   Individual long turn: How to spend your spare time

- *Compare and contrast the two pictures.*
- *Describe the different ways of how someone can spend their spare time.*
- *Give a recommendation as to how someone can best use their free time.*

2   Paired activity: New activities for the not-so-young

The manager of a local community centre has asked you and your partner to draw up a plan to help elderly people to learn how to use modern technology.

Discuss the following aspects:

- *first steps*
- *choice of technology*
- *choice of activities*
- *aims and objectives*
- *consequences for the community*

Decide how to go about this project and agree on a plan.

Support material: Talking about facts

1 Talking about facts

Use the sentence starters below to introduce statements about spare time activities.

1. It is a fact that
....

2. It is true that
....

3. It is noticeable that
....

4. It is obvious that
....

5. The real issue here is that
....

6. It cannot be denied that
....

7. One should note here that
....

8. Let us not forget that
....

2 Improving your word power: Spare time activities

Search online using the key word "spare time activities". Complete the table below with at least seven expressions for each group.

	Team sport	Individual sport	Games	Others
1.				
2.				
3.				
4.				
5.				
6.				
7.				
8.				
9.				
10.				

Topic 9 Consumerism

Tasks

1 Individual long turn: Where to shop

- *Compare and contrast the two pictures.*
- *Describe the advantages and disadvantages of the different shopping styles.*
- *Talk about your personal shopping preferences.*

2 Paired activity: Where to sell

Your school is participating in a project to donate money to a partner school in Guatemala. Your class wants to raise money by selling second-hand items. You and your friend volunteer to find out which method of selling best suits your needs. There are various opportunities: organising a yard sale in your school, selling things through newspaper adverts, using an online platform, selling things to a second-hand store and putting up posters in local supermarkets.

Discuss the following aspects:

- *how much time to spend*
- *possible profit*
- *number of people you can address*
- *fees*
- *how to best get attention*

Decide how your class should proceed. Agree on the two best options.

Support material: Questioning

1 Who

Who ...	had the most impact on your views? can provide supporting evidence for your arguments? should be asked to obtain further information?

2 Where

Where ...	do you stand on this? do you draw the line? do you see this going?

3 When

When ...	did you change your mind in this issue? did you first get in contact with .../hear about ... ? was the last time you ... ?

4 Why

Why ...	is/was ... a good idea? is this an issue for many people? might this be a sensitive point for the people involved?

5 What

What ...	are your motives for getting involved in ... ? lesson do you learn from this development? specific steps would you take to deal with ... ?

6 Which

Which ...	option would be the best for ... ? alternatives are there? is more important: making a huge profit or attracting a lot of publicity?

7 How

How ...	do you feel about this? deeply committed are they to ... ? will you organise this department to avoid repeating that experience?
How far ...	do you trust them/believe in this/go along with this?

Topic 10 Tradition and change

Tasks

1 Individual long turn: Getting around

- *Compare and contrast the two pictures.*
- *Discuss how our lifestyle has changed over the last century.*
- *Analyse the consequences of our modern lifestyle.*

2 Paired activity: Out with the old, in with the new?

In the centre of your town, an old building is to make way for a new office block. At your school, you have decided to take part in the discussion. You and your partner have got the task of producing a poster that outlines the main aspects of such a move. You talk about organising your presentation.

Discuss the following aspects:

- *style and taste*
- *functionality*
- *cost*
- *effect on the neighbourhood*
- *alternative options*

Decide what to put on the poster in order to highlight the problems related to this plan.

Support material: Expressing cause and effect

1 Talking about old and new

a) Group the following words and write them into the appropriate boxes.

brand-new · conservative · contemporary · conventional · dated · current · fashionable · innovative · latest · modern · old-fashioned · old-school · old-style · out-dated · out-of-date · recent · state-of-the-art · traditional · trendy · unfashionable · up-to-date

Old	New

b) Form two groups of synonyms.

to demolish · to destroy · to keep · to modernise · to preserve · to raze to the ground · to rebuild · to reconstruct · to refurbish · to renovate · to repair · to tear down

Synonyms of destruction:

....

....

Synonyms of reconstruction:

....

....

2 Expressing cause and effect

Form a sentence with each of the following phrases.

A possible cause of … . · This has been linked to … . · The result/consequence of … . · A failure to do so might lead to … . · This might cause … . · Consequently … . · Because of this, … . · As a result of this, … . · This will bring about great changes to … . · That would lead to … . · Doing that would mean taking risks … . · What would happen if … ? · Just think of the consequences if … . · If we did that, the consequences would be … .

Topic 11 Transport and tourism

Tasks

1 Individual long turn: Holiday places

- *Compare and contrast the two pictures.*
- *Discuss why people might prefer spending their holidays at the places shown.*
- *Describe the place where you would like to spend your holidays and what you could do there.*

2 Paired activity: The best way to get somewhere

You and your partner plan to travel to France in the holidays. There are various means of transport you could take: the car, a coach, the train or the plane. You talk about which means of transport best suits your needs.

Discuss the following aspects:

- *cost*
- *impact on the environment*
- *speed*
- *convenience*
- *flexibility*

Decide which means of transport to use.

Support material: Requests

1 General requests

> Could I ask you to … ? • I must ask you not to … . • I must insist that … . •
> I would be grateful if you … . • I would like to know … . • It would be very helpful if you … . •
> Would you be kind enough to … ? • Would you mind … ?

2 Refusing a request

> I am afraid I must decline … . • I am afraid I will not be able to … . • I am not in a position to … . •
> I'm sorry, but I have to reject … . • I can't possibly manage it. •
> I regret to have to inform you that … . • It is out of the question for me to … . •
> It will be very difficult for me to … . • You cannot expect me to … .

3 Asking for clarification

How to express lack of understanding

> I beg your pardon, but I don't quite understand. • I don't quite see what you mean. •
> I don't quite see what you're getting at. • I'm not quite sure I can follow you. •
> I'm not quite sure I know what you mean. • I'm not sure I got your point. •
> Sorry, I didn't get your point. • Sorry, I didn't quite hear what you said.

How to ask for clarification

> Are you claiming … ? • Are you saying that … ? • Can you be more specific? • Can you clarify that
> for me? • Can you share some examples? • Can you spin that concept out for us? • Could you be
> more explicit? • Could you be more specific, please? • Could you clarify that, please? • Could you
> explain what you mean by … ? • Could you give us an example? • Could you put it differently,
> please? • Could you repeat please? • Could you say that again, please? • Do you mean … ? • How
> did you reach that conclusion? • How does that statement apply to … ? • I wonder if you could say
> that in a different way. • So you are saying … ? • What are the implications of that statement? •
> What are you implying? • What do you mean by … ? • What do you really mean? • What does that
> mean? • Why do you think that? • Would you elaborate on that, please?

4 Clarify your ideas

> I mean … . • In other words, … . • My point is that … . • That's to say … . • That's why … . •
> The reason is that … . • Therefore … . • Try to see it from my point of view. •
> What I really mean is … . • What I'm getting at is … . • What I'm trying to say is … .

Topic 12 Cultural aspects of English-speaking countries

Tasks

1 Individual long turn: Cultural similarities, cultural differences

- *Compare and contrast the two pictures.*
- *Analyse the various cultural aspects of life in Britain.*
- *Comment on the way in which cultural differences can be dealt with.*

2 Paired activity: Getting to know others

For a school project on cultural awareness, people in your area should be asked about their background. Together with a partner you are supposed to carry out the survey. With your partner, you plan the questionnaire, its content and how to organise the survey.

Discuss the following aspects:

- *aims of the whole project*
- *strategy to make people talk*
- *questions to ask*
- *aspects to exclude*
- *organising the survey*

Decide how to organise the survey and agree on a draft for the questionnaire.

Support material: Presenting ideas

1 Presenting your ideas

Use the phrases below to introduce and link the statements about cultural similarities and differences in Britain.

Starting	Continuing	Concluding
First … . Firstly, … . In the first place … . First of all, there's the question of … . I want to begin by looking at … . Let's look at the general idea first … . Secondly, … . Thirdly, … .	As far as … is/are concerned … . Furthermore … . In addition to … . In addition to this there is … . As well as … . One must also remember that … . Then there's … . At this point … . In this context … . To return to our main issue … . Besides that, … . Another thing is … .	Finally … . Finally, I'd like to say … .

Britain has always had close relationships with her former colonies.

There are strong immigrant communities all over Britain, especially in London and bigger cities.

For many the British Monarchy is the link between various cultures and backgrounds.

A number of members of immigrant communities have climbed the social ladder and are now well-respected lawyers, doctors, academics or politicians.

Many immigrants have brought their own customs and traditions which can be seen in many ways.

It can be said that immigrants play a major role in public life in Britain.

In many towns and cities immigrants contribute to local communities by running corner shops and providing services that would otherwise not be available.

Topic 13 Art and culture

Tasks

1 Individual long turn: The many faces of art

- *Compare and contrast the two pictures.*
- *Describe what makes these two women artists, according to your view.*
- *Discuss which qualities or talents artists should have.*

2 Paired activity: Let's enjoy some art!

You and your friend want to enjoy some art at the weekend. There are various things you could do: visit an art gallery, go to a classical concert, go to the theatre, go to the cinema or see a sculpture garden. You talk about where to go.

Discuss the following aspects:

- *entry fee*
- *personal preferences*
- *background information needed*
- *time*
- *location*

Decide how you would like to spend your weekend.

Support material: Expressing intentions

1 Expressing intentions

Asking what someone intends or wants
I would like to know what you want to do. • I'm not quite sure what you intend by that. • What do you intend to do? • What do you propose to do about … ? • Why do you want to … of all things?

Saying what you intend
I am (really) determined to … . • I have no intention whatsoever of … . • I just wanted to … . • I meant to … . • I'm planning to … . • I'm toying with the idea of … . • One of these days I'm going to … .

Saying what you (don't) want or like
I don't feel inclined to … . • I don't intend to … . • I feel like … . • I have decided to … . • I have made up my mind to … . • I hope I'll … . • I really want everyone to … . • I'd really like to … . • It is very important that … . • My dearest wish is to … . • There's absolutely no question of my … .

2 Suggesting

Asking for suggestions
Does anyone have a better suggestion? • What am I/is one supposed to do? • What would you do if you were me?

Suggesting	
I think you should …	agree with the decision … .
I'd advise you to …	be more specific … .
Is there any reason why we shouldn't …	carry on … .
It might not be a bad idea to …	clarify that for us … .
Let's …	elaborate on that … .
Perhaps you ought to …	emphasise … .
Why don't you just …	examine that further … .
Why not …	explain what you mean by … .
You could always …	put it differently … .
You mustn't forget to …	reconsider … .
You would certainly be advised to …	repeat … .
You'd have no choice but to …	say that again.
Have you considered …	check**ing** the figures?
Have you ever thought of …	shar**ing** some examples?
How about …	start**ing** now?
How would you feel about …	stopp**ing** … ?
May I suggest …	support**ing** … ?
What about …	tackl**ing** it this way?

Topic 14 Media

Tasks

1 Individual long turn: News

- *Compare and contrast the two pictures.*
- *Analyse the characteristics of modern communication.*
- *Explain why modern media are so important in society.*

2 Paired activity: Internet information

The internet offers enormous amounts of information which need to be processed by its users. As a young person, you have grown up with the internet and its blessings. Your head teacher has therefore asked you and your partner to make a list of recommendations for the youngest pupils in your school.

Discuss the following aspects:

- *reliability of information*
- *ways to detect manipulation*
- *measures to avoid being manipulated*
- *guidelines on internet security*
- *activities in school to highlight this problem*

Decide which recommendations to give to the young pupils. Agree on three.

Support material: Refusing permission and presenting solutions

1 Refusing permission

Use phrases from the list below and form recommendations with regard to media use.

You can't (possibly) … .	I don't allow you to … .
I (absolutely) forbid you to … .	I cannot accept that … .
I'd rather you didn't … .	I mustn't … .
I don't want … to … .	My … has forbidden me to … .
It is forbidden to … .	It is (strictly) prohibited … .
We don't need to … until … .	I am authorised to … .

2 Presenting solutions: Internet access at school

Combine the phrases in the left column with appropriate phrases from the right one. Find at least two options for each introductory phrase. Make sure you use the correct form.

What would work out best is if we …	code to access the internet in school.
What we could do is …	settings for internet access.
Couldn't we simply change the …	put on a workshop for internet users.
As I see it, the solution is clear: we need to …	inform parents about the dangers of the internet.
I wonder if we could change the …	ban mobile phones in school.
Why don't we …	revise/change our policies.
We should not forget to …	present the benefits and the dangers of the internet.

3 Vocabulary revision: Media

Go through the list and find a fourth word related to the other three in that line. Each of them refers to a form of media.

1. volume	cover	hardback	*book*
2. internet forum	newsgroup	blog	
3. supplement	headline	editorial	
4. presenter	phone-in programme	feature	
5. coverage	anchor	documentary	

Topic 15 Communication

Tasks

1 **Individual long turn: How we stay in touch**

- *Compare and contrast the two pictures.*
- *Describe the advantages and disadvantages of mobile phones.*
- *Suggest rules for a responsible use of mobile technology in public.*

2 **Paired activity: Using mobile phones in class**

The principal of your school plans to ban the use of mobile phones in class. As student representatives, you and your partner are asked to join a discussion with teachers and parents. You prepare for the discussion together: one of you is strongly in favour of the proposition; one of you is strongly against it.

Discuss the following aspects:

- *potential for disruption*
- *opportunities for learning*
- *social inequality*
- *theft*
- *health issues*

Decide which arguments to use in the discussion with the principal. Agree on three.

Support material: Generalising and quantifying

1 Generalising

When you make generalisations rather than say something is a fact, you will sound less sure of yourself and therefore more open to other people's opinions and ideas.

All in all, using mobile phones has more advantages than disadvantages.
All things considered, the situation could be much worse.
The phone reception was quite good, actually **almost always** flawless.
As a (general) rule, if you haven't used an app for 6 months, you don't need it.
But **broadly speaking** the health issues related to mobile phones are not really worrying.
It has taken us a long time to accept that the choices made by the government were, **by and large**, the right choices.
For the most part it has been comparatively cheap and convenient to use social networking sites.
Generally (speaking), the traditional phone system is unable to meet current demands.
Society often **has a tendency to** reject technical progress at first.
It may be true in **a large number of cases**, and it may be false in an equally large number.
Offensive language has no place in e-mails in particular and in communication **in general**.
In some cases, parents are forced to choose between giving in to peer pressure and turning their child into a social outcast.
In most cases, people do not care about security measures on the web.
Travelling in a foreign country leads to higher phone costs, but **in my experience** even the experienced traveller needs to stay in touch with his family and friends from time to time.
It goes without saying that we are proud of what our company has achieved.
I've often found that the opposite works.
More often than not, the decision is not so simple.
Most of the time, young teenagers are not even taken seriously.
My morning routine **normally** begins with checking my mailbox and looking at my Facebook page.
On the whole, parents should work on protecting their children's privacy.
Overall, phone costs have gone up by more than the inflation rate.
Taking everything into account, the people at the call centre do a great job.
Young phone users are **typically** interested in using instant messaging services rather than e-mail.
A new study has found that people who use their mobiles regularly **usually** spend more money on online shopping than other groups.

2 Quantifying

Expressions of quantity are placed before nouns and express "how much" or "how many".

Today, there's **a (large) number of** people that don't have desktop computers.
There are, however, **a couple of** lessons here for everyone.
I would like to make **a few** points regarding reduced prices of smartphones.
Smartphones fail in **a great deal of** rural areas, as there's no data service at all.
I'm unfortunately **a little** bit of a phone junkie myself.
Many young people are entering the job market without the right communication skills.
Being without a mobile phone can be one of the **most** miserable experiences imaginable for some.
Learning how to use mobile communication was **much** easier for me than it was for my parents.
Plenty of people miss their share of happiness, not because they never found it, but because they didn't stop to enjoy it.
They do spend **(quite) a lot of** money on new devices.
The question of how much internet control is necessary has been hotly debated for **several** years.
The majority of smartphone owners in the US don't download any apps.

Topic 16 Nature and the environment

Tasks

1 **Individual long turn: Playing with fire**

- *Compare and contrast the two pictures.*
- *Discuss what has changed in human behaviour over the last few decades.*
- *Suggest measures to improve the situation.*

2 Paired activity: Beware of the roads

A new road scheme in your area is threatening the wildlife in your neighbourhood. However, only few people seem to be interested in this issue. Together with a friend, you have decided to raise awareness of the issue in your neighbourhood.

Discuss the following aspects:

- *activities to raise awareness*
- *funding*
- *objectives of your campaign*
- *alternative plans for the road scheme*
- *other contributors to contact*

Decide how to go about this campaign.

Support material: Expressing dimensions

1 **Revising vocabulary: The environment – 64 useful words and phrases**

a) Go through this list of words and make sure you know all of them.
b) Form sentences in which you either describe environmental problems or in which you make suggestions
   as to how to protect the environment. Use as many items from the list as possible.

Example:

Untreated sewage is harmful to the wildlife in rivers.

acid rain	to die out	hydraulic power plant	to recycle
to affect	to diminish	incinerator	to reduce
atmosphere	drought	industrial waste	renewable
to be exposed to	to dump	landfill site	reusable
to be harmful	ecology	to lead to	sewage
to become extinct	ecosystem	marine life	soil
biodegradable	emission	natural gas	to threaten
biodiversity	to emit	ocean	toxic waste
biosphere	endangered species	ozone	untreated
carbon dioxide	energy-efficient	ozone layer	urbanisation
carbon monoxide	erosion	poison	waste disposal
to cause	exhaust fumes	polar icecaps	waste paper
to combat	flooding	pollution	water treatment
to contaminate	global warming	power station	wildlife
to destroy	greenhouse effect	to protect	wind energy
detergent	to harm	rainforest	wind farm

2 **Expressing dimensions**

Take sentences from the previous task and combine them with items from below.

all over the world   almost all   almost every second person

approximately   everywhere   it is estimated that   a large amount of

mainly   the majority of people   many   most   much   nearly

primarily   rarely   roughly   a small minority   wherever you go

Topic 17 New technologies

Tasks

1 Individual long turn: Household chores now and then

- *Compare and contrast the two pictures.*
- *Explain how technology facilitates everyone's daily lives.*
- *Discuss why you would/wouldn't use devices like the one shown in the picture on the right.*

2 Paired activity: The most important inventions ever

The local museum plans to host an exhibition on new technologies. You and your partner, volunteers for the museum, have been asked to design one room of the exhibition. This room should show the three most important inventions that have ever been created. With your partner, you brainstorm a number of inventions.

Discuss the following aspects:

- *grade of innovation/creativity*
- *relevance for people's daily lives*
- *economic success*
- *ecological impact*
- *personal preferences/interests*

Decide which inventions should be shown in the exhibition. Agree on three.

Support material: Referring and emphasising

1 Introducing a statement

(Well,) I feel that … I'd like to say that … In my view/opinion … It seems to me that … To begin with … We all know that …	parents shouldn't allow their children to use the internet freely. a dishwasher is the most important household appliance. children should also consider the environmental footprint of their gadgets. a good TV set is more important than travelling. high school students are more open to new technologies. engineers should make a higher salary than managers. television is the leading cause of violence in today's society. the government should pay for digital infrastructure.

2 Referring to what has been said

As far as downloading movies from the internet without paying **is concerned**, this is definitely not OK, even if you can get away with it.

As for fines: They have never had any good effect.

As to people who waste energy: They should definitely pay high taxes for electricity.

As you said, automatic household appliances are more convenient than we might think.

Didn't you mean to say that all communication should be free?

If I understood you correctly, you said there should be no fines for breaking the law.

Talking about copyright: I can't imagine a single situation where a breach of copyright is necessary.

3 Emphasising

And besides, we should be paying fewer taxes, not more taxes.

And, on top of (all) that, practicality is more important than design.

Don't forget that everyone is basically interested in new things.

First and foremost, people should be able to take part in new developments.

Furthermore, technical expertise is a matter of personal interest.

I would even go so far as to say (that) all students should be enabled to use text processors for free.

In order to emphasise Javier's argument, I would like to remind you of the idea that someday people will be controlled everywhere all the time.

Let me point out that boys and girls must get the same access to the net.

Let us make it clear that many new machines lead to a reduction of the workforce.

Let us not forget that new technologies will not solve our problems unless we change our lifestyle.

Most importantly, we must realise that machines aren't more important than happiness.

Remember, the real issue at stake is that bullying on the net should be illegal.

Take the case of motivation: People work better if they have more spare time.

That proves my point, that access to modern technology is in fact a form of power.

The point I'm trying to make is that high school shouldn't be mandatory for everyone.

This does not mean that we have forgotten how to socialise with each other, **but** that we are too dependent on computers and smartphones.

What we need is better professional training.

What's more, it will be an improvement on the present situation.

Topic 18 Plans and future opportunities

Tasks

1 Individual long turn: Family or career?

- *Compare and contrast the two pictures.*
- *Speculate about the future careers of the people in the two pictures.*
- *Discuss the importance of education for the future of young people.*

2 Paired activity: A year abroad

You are about to graduate and not sure if you should go on to university or look for a job. A counsellor at your school recommends taking a gap year. You talk about this suggestion with your best friend, who thinks this is a great idea and wants to come with you.

Discuss the following aspects:

- *convincing your parents*
- *financial considerations*
- *coping with problems abroad*
- *consequences for your careers*
- *expectations*

Decide what to do.

Support material: Expressing certainty

1 Expressing certainty

a) Use chunks from both columns and make up statements about future opportunities.

1. There's no doubt that …	D	**A**	a job should also be rewarding, not just well-paid.
2. It's absolutely certain that …		**B**	a career in business is what most people want.
3. I am absolutely certain that …		**C**	having enough spare time is more important than a career.
4. I am sure that …		**Ø**	this job will pay more than any other.
5. As I was saying, …		**E**	stress-related illnesses are on the rise.
6. I'm totally sure that …		**F**	I will have a family before long.
7. As a rule, …		**G**	I will not be able to stand the pressure.
8. There is no doubt that …		**H**	women are underpaid.
9. After all, …		**I**	loyalty is one of the key features of an employee.
10. What I wanted to say is that …		**J**	soft skills are most important.
11. I am convinced that …		**K**	managers have a lot of responsibility.
12. Undoubtedly, …		**L**	competition is vital in modern business.

b) Write down one statement for each of the sentence starters.

2 Referring to the future

Make up a short statement about your personal future, using as many of the phrases below as possible.

in the future	after school
in the next few years	after leaving school
next month	before going to university
next year	after graduating
in a few months	after my graduation
in a few years	later
in ten years from now	before long
in summer	in five years time

Topic 19 Intercultural and social aspects

Tasks

1 Individual long turn: Food for thought

- *Compare and contrast the two pictures.*
- *Describe the problems of homeless people.*
- *Analyse what can be done to help homeless people.*

2 Paired activity: Being an ambassador for your country

You have won a competition organised by the United Nations and have now been invited to New York to a worldwide congress of teenagers. During the conference, you are required to give a presentation on your country. Together with your friend, you prepare for the presentation and brainstorm a number of cultural aspects of your country.

Discuss the following aspects:

- *the importance of family and friends*
- *cultural activities (e.g. films, songs, theatre) that you enjoy and that reflect and influence your culture*
- *popular places to spend one's free time*
- *health issues*
- *preserving the environment*

Decide which points to include in the presentation. Agree on three.

Support material: Criticising and contradicting

1 Challenging an argument

I can't accept those assumptions/your argument. • I don't see how you can argue like that. • I don't see how you can predict/assume that. • It simply/just wouldn't work in practice. • Prove it! • What facts and figures are you using to support your argument? • What has that got to do with it/the issue? • Where are the facts? • Where's your proof? • You haven't convinced me yet! • I'm sorry, but I think your argument is flawed.

2 Expressing criticism

Criticism is without a doubt needed in lively discussions, but it also has to be balanced by consent and praise. Expressing criticism in a positive way, rather than being constantly negative, creates an energy boost rather than a drain.

As a matter of fact, I think that's completely misleading. • But you have failed to account for the rising costs in social services. • I don't feel you've understood the main problem of the people concerned. • I don't see how you can argue for increased government funding when the resources are limited. • I don't think you realise how serious the situation is. • I think you're missing the point. • If I understand you correctly, you would reduce public spending on social programmes for the homeless? • It's ridiculous to suggest that there's no solution. • Look, what about the rising number of homeless? • That's all very well but what about the legal aspects? • Very interesting. So how exactly do you propose to do it? • Well that doesn't get us very far, does it? • You seem to have forgotten the costs of European unity.

3 Contradicting

But don't you think that everybody is entitled to access the same resources? • But that's not fair. • Do you really believe that? • Don't get me wrong, but I think you should take all new scientific developments into account. • I'm sorry, but I don't see it like that. • I'm afraid I don't agree. • I'm against constantly putting all the blame on schools/teachers. • Not at all. In fact food prices have been on the rise for many months now. • On the contrary: This law was passed decades ago. • Quite the opposite. • Well, actually current studies have revealed that this is no longer true.

4 Correcting

… are completely groundless. • I think it should be … rather than … . • I think you've got the numbers wrong. • I would like to point out one small error in … . • I'm sorry but this is not correct. • In (actual) fact … . • In reality … . • This is (simply) not in accordance with the facts. • It is not a question of … but of … . • The truth is that … .

Topic 20 Growing up

Tasks

1   **Individual long turn: The pains of growing up**

- *Compare and contrast the two pictures.*
- *Discuss different circumstances under which children grow up today.*
- *Explain the advantages and disadvantages of the way in which people are brought up.*

2   **Paired activity: Our problems**

As an introduction to a parents' evening on teenage problems, you and your partner have been invited to give a short presentation in which you should depict the most important aspects of adolescence from your point of view. As you will only have a few minutes, you have to decide which issues are the most important ones and which ones can be left out.

Discuss the following aspects:

- *aspects related to school*
- *self-esteem*
- *relationships with your peers and your family*
- *possible medical conditions*
- *consequences for one's career*

Decide which aspects you are going to focus on. Agree on three.

Support material: Expressing doubt

1 **Reacting to statements: Expressing doubt**

a) Match the following sentence halves. In some cases, more than one solution is possible.

1. I'm not sure if parents should …	G	**A**	are always right.
2. I'm not convinced by what adults …		**B**	be loyal to you in such a situation.
3. I've got reservations about …		**C**	discuss every detail of their private lives.
4. I think teenagers are young adults after all and …		**D**	discussing everything with my parents.
5. I doubt if it helps to …		**E**	handle their affairs properly.
6. That does not necessarily mean that parents …		**F**	have to decide for themselves.
7. There is no reason to assume that teenagers always …		**G**	interfere when children have problems at school.
8. I wonder if it is good to …		**H**	is going to last.
9. Are you really sure that your friends would …		**I**	say about their teenage years.
10. I have my doubts that such a friendship …		**J**	tell your teachers about such an incident.

b) Use the sentence starters below and rephrase the sentences from above.

They have their doubts that … .

Well, if you ask me I think that … .

I'm not at all convinced that …

You must admit that … .

I have my reservations that … .

Well, I'm not too sure if … .

It is still not certain whether … .

I think it is debatable if … .

I still don't know exactly how … .

I'm not sure whether … .

I would be very surprised if … .

It is still impossible to say if … .

After all I don't think that … .

You must admit that … .

I doubt if … .

Topic 21 Politics and public institutions

Tasks

1 **Individual long turn: To vote or not to vote**

 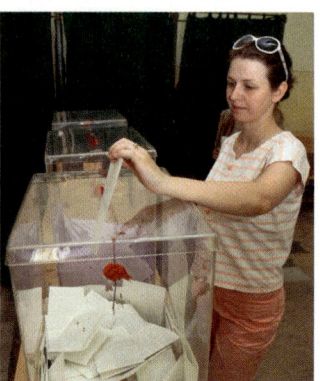

- *Compare and contrast the two pictures.*
- *Describe which qualities are needed to occupy a leading role in a country.*
- *Discuss why voting is or isn't a right that everyone should appreciate.*

2 **Paired activity: Running for students' representative**

There will be elections for the students' representatives at your school in a few weeks. You and your friend are not sure whether to run for the office as a candidate or not.

Discuss the following aspects:

- *tasks*
- *job description*
- *responsibility*
- *fame among fellow students*
- *pros and cons*

Decide whether or not to run for students' representative in the election.

Support material: Persuading and offering

1 Persuading

In a discussion, you often try to convince your partner of a belief, position or course of action by using suitable arguments or questions.

Another thing … . • But actually … . • But can't you see … . • But in fact … . • But the real question is … . • Don't misunderstand me, … . • Even so, … . • Have you thought of … ? • In a case like this … . • In this sort of situation … . • It's in your interests to … . • Let me put it another way. • Let's face it, there won't be a better … . • Look at it this way: … . • Many people think … . • Not only that, but … . • Not to mention the fact that … . • Oh, I almost forgot … . • Perhaps I should mention … . • Plus the fact that … . • Possibly, but … . • Some people say … . • Surely it would make more sense to … . • That would be great, except … . • That's the reason why … . • The fact of the matter is … . • The point is … . • The reason is … . • To start with … . • What I mean is … . • What's more, … . • Why not change track/start all over again? • Wouldn't it be better to … ? • Yes, but … . • You could always consider … . • You must admit that it's an attractive proposal. • You'd better take the opportunity now. • You've probably heard that … .

2 Offering

With the following phrases you can offer services or goods to other people or suggest a course of action to follow.

Can I get you a copy of the report?
Have another attempt at describing the situation!
How about asking the experts for their evaluation?
How would you like me to present the results of the survey?
I could rephrase my last comment **if you like**.
I could always return to the previous subject.
I would be glad to take care of this matter.
I would be more than happy to share my findings with you.
I'll happily agree to your proposal.
It would be a great pleasure to discuss these issues with you.
Please allow me to introduce our host.
Please feel free to contact me whenever needed.
Shall I start by explaining how it all started?
We could have a break at that point.
We should like to pay attention to the needs of all people concerned.
We would be very happy to support you in this matter.
What if I had copies made of the report?
Why don't I take the minutes today?
Would you like to have a look around before we start?

Topic 22 Globalisation

Tasks

1 **Individual long turn: Think globally, act locally**

- *Compare and contrast the two pictures.*
- *Discuss the effects of globalisation on our lives.*
- *Speculate about future developments in this area.*

2 **Paired activity: Partying in a globalised world**

At school you have learned about the effects of globalisation and our consumer habits. As you and your partner want to organise a farewell party at school, you have decided to do it without generating negative effects on society or the environment.

Discuss the following aspects:

- *food and drinks*
- *personal contributions*
- *energy management*
- *dress code*
- *activities*

Decide which measures would be the most effective ones. Agree on three.

Support material: Recommending and referring

1 Recommending action

Use the phrases below to give recommendations with respect to the negative effects of globalisation by combining them with words and phrases from the yellow box. Tick (✓) the phrases you have used.

should be abolished should be reviewed should be reduced

should be changed should be introduced should be observed

should be provided shouldn't ought to are not supposed to

is/were better if the best way to It is necessary to … .

It is of great importance that … . have the obligation to needs to be done

It would be most desirable if … . should be considered The main priority is to … .

❑ to buy goods from local producers	❑ to negotiate fair agreements
❑ child labour	❑ outsourcing
❑ to exploit people in developing countries	❑ to pay fair wages
❑ fair cooperation	❑ to purchase goods from certified producers
❑ fair-trade products	❑ to respect workers' rights
❑ global trade rules	❑ to support people in developing countries
❑ health and safety regulations	❑ sweatshops
❑ to import goods from	❑ to take advantage of cheap labour
❑ to impose taxes on	❑ trade barriers
❑ international trade agreements	❑ unemployment
❑ multinational companies	❑ working conditions in factories

Example:

> The main priority is to negotiate fair trade agreements between the Western world and developing countries.

2 Referring to a previous point

Use the following phrases and form statements that refer to a previous point in your conversation.

As for … .	As to … .
Didn't you mean to say that … ?	Talking about … .
As you said (before), … .	As far as … is concerned … .
Could you say that again, please?	If I understood you correctly, you said … .
As I mentioned earlier, … .	As we saw earlier … .

Topic 23 Social groups and minorities

Tasks

1 Individual long turn: Inside out

- *Compare and contrast the two pictures.*
- *Speculate about the reasons why some people appear to live on the fringes of society.*
- *Suggest a course of action to work towards an "inclusive" society.*

2 Paired activity: Creating an inclusive school

This year, your school is focusing on working towards an "inclusive" school, i.e. making sure that fellow students with special needs get all the support they need in order to take part in all activities. You and your partner are members of a focus group that is preparing the project. Brainstorm what it takes to create an inclusive school.

Discuss the following aspects:

- *transport*
- *getting around the school*
- *special facilities*
- *equipment for supporting learners*
- *creating a community*

Decide which suggestions you are going to make to the principal. Agree on three.

Support material: Changing the subject and interrupting

1 Changing the subject

Before I forget … . • By the way … . • Changing the subject for a minute … . • Could we change the topic? • I just thought of something. • I know this is changing the subject but … . • I know this isn't really what we're talking about, but … . • I would prefer not to discuss this issue with you. • Incidentally, … . • Oh, there's something else I wanted to ask you. • Oh, while I remember … . • Sorry to cut you off, but … . • Speaking about/of … . • That reminds me of … . • That's funny, because something similar … . • This has got nothing to do with what we're talking about, but … . • This is not the best topic right now. • What about … ?

2 Changing your mind

To change one's mind
to amend • to consider again • to have second thoughts • to reassess • to recheck • to re-evaluate • to rethink • to revise • to see sth. in a new light • to take another look at sth. • to think better of • to think sth. over • to think twice

So he**'s changed his mind about** people who do not join in with the crowd.
She**'s gradually shifted her opinion** on the value of inclusive education.
I**'ve come round to thinking** it's a good idea.
After some thought, I decided that it was worth doing/worth a try.
On second thought, I don't know if it could work.

3 Conceding

In a discussion it might be necessary for you to say that you accept or do not deny the truth or existence of something – you concede.

Although some people may say … . • At least one can say that … . • Basically, I agree with … , but … . • But the fact remains that … . • Certainly … , but I would still … . • Doubtless … , but … . • I agree with you up to a point, but … . • I see what you mean, but … . • I suppose you're right, but … . • It cannot be denied that … , but … . • One must also say that … . • One must admit that … , but one … . • One should question whether … . • One should raise the point that … . • Well, if you put it like that … . • Without wishing to belittle … , one … .

4 Interrupting

Interrupting
Just a second. • Now look here, … . • That reminds me … . • Wait a minute. • Well, I'd just like to say … . • What did you just say? • If I could just interrupt you there … .

Stopping the other person from interrupting
Before you interrupt me, I would like to … . • Just let me finish my point, please.

Topic 24 Rules, regulations and legal matters

Tasks

1 Individual long turn: Don't do that!

- *Compare and contrast the two pictures.*
- *Analyse the meaning of these signs and the reasons why they have been put up.*
- *Explain what you think about such signs and rules in general.*

2 Paired activity: School rules

As you and your partner are among the oldest students in your school, the head of your school has asked you to draw up a new set of general rules for your fellow students. These rules should become the house rules in the next school year and should take the interests of all pupils – young and old – into account.

Discuss the following aspects:

- *classroom work*
- *general behaviour towards fellow students and staff*
- *behaviour during the breaks*
- *ways to deal with the equipment of the school*
- *emergency procedures*

Decide which recommendations to present to the head of your school. Agree on three.

Support material: Concluding

1 Community rules of a website

Look at the rules of a web community and find reasons why they have been put into place.

	Stay on topic.
Keep it civil and respectful.	Keep it legal.
	Don't be abusive towards others.
No spam.	Observe copyright and trademark law.
	No impersonations.
Protect your privacy.	Respect the privacy of others.
	Don't upload or post inappropriate content.

2 Concluding

Use the sentence starters on the left and match them with the chunks on the right to create meaningful sentences.

1.	In conclusion, it is clear that …	D	A	rules stop people from being creative.
2.	On the whole, …		B	people need rules to avoid problems.
3.	We have put that on one side for the time being because …		C	everybody should be mature enough to know what to do.
4.	Opinion was divided on the issue because…		D	rules help people to get on well with each other.
5.	In general, we have to say that …		E	unfortunately people are too immature to respect each other.
6.	We finally reached a compromise over …		F	people don't need rules as long as they treat each other with respect.
7.	You said that you agreed with the idea in general that …		G	people would have lost interest in the site if there had not been strict rules.
8.	What I'm saying is, we should keep in mind that …		H	every community needs rules to function properly.
9.	In short, …		I	rules can be a great help.
10.	In brief, …		J	most people like guidelines.
11.	In other words, …		K	a community with strict rules can also be problematic.
12.	Let me put it this way, …		L	rules give people a chance to interfere.
13.	To sum up, …		M	the issue of rules.
14.	I think that just about sums it up because …		N	only a few people would have problems following the rules of the site.

Topics   Prime Time 5 bis 8

Topic	Vorkommen in Prime Time 5 bis 8

1. Relationships and social networks	**Prime Time 5**
	Unit 3: *Angela* (S. 34)
	Unit 4: The Baby Borrowers (S. 48)
	            Sorry, you're wrong! (S. 54)
	            How to: Argue politely (S. 54)
	Unit 7: Dignity for all? (S. 88)
	            Tolerance and respect (S. 93)
	            Heroes (S. 95)
	            The Civil Rights Movement (S. 97)
	Prime Time 5 Transition
	Unit 5: The Baby Borrowers (S. 63)
	            Sorry, you're wrong! (S. 68)
	            How to: Argue politely (S. 68)
	Unit 9: *Angela* (S. 119)
	Prime Time 6
	Unit 1: Friendship (S. 8)
	Unit 6: "She doesn't speak" by Marita van der Vyver (S. 78)
	Unit 7: *Martin Lukes: Who Moved My BlackBerry?* by Lucy Kellaway (S. 94)
	Prime Time 7
	Unit 2: People with special needs (S. 30)
	Unit 3: *Snow falling on cedars* by David Guterson (S. 45)
	Unit 5: "Life is fine" by Langston Hughes (S. 67)
	            "Arranged marriage" by Chitra Banerjee Divakaruni (S. 68)
	            Male voices – Andrew Allan (S. 80)
	Unit 6: Gandhi – Father to a nation, stranger to his son (S. 89)
	Unit 9: The Mattani family: Three generations, two cultures (S. 136)
	Prime Time 8
	Unit 6: Single and happy: It's the freemales (S. 70)

2. Home and surroundings	**Prime Time 6**
	Unit 2: Caribbean London (S. 20)
	            Video: Caribbeans in London (S. 21)
	            Video: The Notting Hill Carnival (S. 28)
	Unit 6: Apartheid (S. 76)
	            "She doesn't speak" by Marita van der Vyver (S. 78)
	            What to see and do (S. 83)
	Unit 7: The world of Google (S. 90)
	Prime Time 7
	Unit 3: London – The Great Wen (S. 36)
	            Only Gaelic? (S. 42)
	Unit 5: *Into the wild* by Jon Krakauer (S. 74)
	Unit 8: Street art (S. 114)
	            Architecture (S. 120)
	Unit 9: "In my country" by Jackie King (S. 132)
	            Lord Morris of Handsworth (S. 132)
	            A sense of community (S. 139)
	Prime Time 8
	Unit 1: "Westering Home" by Bernard O'Donoghue (S. 8)
	Unit 2: Housing 2.0 (S. 22)

Topic	Vorkommen in Prime Time 5 bis 8
3. Fashion and trends	**Prime Time 5 Transition** Unit 3: Shopping (S. 42) Unit 4: Unusual hobbies (S. 50) Geocaching (S. 52) **Prime Time 6** Unit 10: Living dolls (S. 130) *Uglies* by Scott Westerfeld (S. 135) The history of tattoos (S. 138) The history of the T-shirt (S. 140) Skincare for men (S. 141) **Prime Time 8** Unit 7: Spend it, spend it, spend more (S. 80) Shop 'til you drop (S. 82)
4. Nutrition, health and welfare	**Prime Time 5 Transition** Unit 3: Eating out (S. 38) **Prime Time 6** Unit 1: Teenage pregnancies (S. 13) Unit 2: Looking at food in the UK (S. 30) Unit 6: What to see and do (S. 83) Unit 10: *Uglies* by Scott Westerfeld (S. 135) The history of tattoos (S. 138) Skincare for men (S. 141) **Prime Time 7** Unit 2: You are what you eat (S. 22) No smoking (S. 26) People with special needs (S. 30) Unit 5: Stress management (S. 77) Coping with stress (S. 78) Exam stress (S. 81) **Prime Time 8** Unit 8: How stem cells can turn back the biological clock (S. 94) Genetic modification: Food (S. 97) Designer food (S. 98)
5. Sports (including social and economic aspects)	**Prime Time 5 Transition** Unit 4: Sports (S. 48) Geocaching (S. 52) **Prime Time 6** Unit 9: eSports (S. 118) Extreme sports (S. 120) Cheerleading: An extreme sport? (S. 121)
6. School and education	**Prime Time 5** Unit 1: The world speaks English (S. 9) Unit 9: Work experience (S. 115) **Prime Time 5 Transition** Unit 1: How to learn English (S. 12) Unit 7: Work experience (S. 89) **Prime Time 8** Unit 10: Lifelong learning (S. 114) School alternatives (S. 116) Opportunities: Taking a break (S. 118) Applying for university (S. 120) Adult education (S. 122) Don't reduce student loans (S. 124) Brightworks (S. 125)

Topic	Vorkommen in Prime Time 5 bis 8

7. The world of work	**Prime Time 5**
	Unit 1: Just another pizza order in Manhattan (S. 10)
	Unit 2: Now that's what I call living! (S. 21)
	Unit 9: The world of work (S. 112)
	        Jobs, jobs, jobs … (S. 114)
	        Work experience (S. 115)
	        Applying for a job (S. 117)
	        Working environments (S. 120)
	        Making a good impression at a job interview (S. 122)
	Prime Time 5 Transition
	Unit 1: Just another pizza order in Manhattan (S. 10)
	Unit 2: Now that's what I call living! (S. 26)
	Unit 7: The world of work (S. 86)
	        Jobs, jobs, jobs … (S. 88)
	        Work experience (S. 89)
	        Applying for a job (S. 91)
	        Working environments (S. 94)
	        Making a good impression at a job interview (S. 96)
	Prime Time 6
	Unit 5: International outsourcing (S. 68)
	Unit 7: The world of Google (S. 90)
	        Tips for job interviews (S. 91)
	        Tips for young job seekers (S. 93)
	        Martin Lukes: Who Moved My BlackBerry? by Lucy Kellaway (S. 94)
	        Telephoning at work (S. 97)
	        Wave goodbye to the nine to five (S. 101)
	Unit 9: Cheerleading: An extreme sport? (S. 121)
	Prime Time 7
	Unit 2: People with special needs (S. 30)
	Unit 4: Entering adulthood (S. 56)
	        Britain's lost talent (S. 58)
	        Working teenagers (S. 59)
	Unit 5: Stress management (S. 77)
	        Coping with stress (S. 78)
	        Exam stress (S. 81)
	Prime Time 8
	Unit 4: Canada: Attentive acupuncturist (S. 44)
	        United States: An immigrant's long journey (S. 46)
	        Canada: New pioneers (S. 52)
	Unit 5: Seeds of peace (S. 58)
	Unit 6: Volunteering: Network for Good (S. 68)
	        A day in my life (S. 74)
	Unit 7: Spend it, spend it, spend more (S. 80)
	        Shop 'til you drop (S. 82)
	Unit 10: Lifelong learning (S. 114)
	        School alternatives (S. 116)
	        Opportunities: Taking a break (S. 118)
	        Applying for university (S. 120)

8. Hobbies and spare time activities	**Prime Time 5** Unit 8: Producing your own music (S. 100) Unit 10: Publishing one's own writing (S. 132) **Prime Time 5 Transition** Unit 3: The trip of a lifetime (S. 34)

Topic	Vorkommen in Prime Time 5 bis 8
8. Hobbies and spare time activities	Eating out (S. 38) Shopping (S. 42) Unit 4: Sports (S. 48) Doing something sensible (S. 49) Unusual hobbies (S. 50) Geocaching (S. 52) Unit 6: Producing your own music (S. 74) Unit 10: Publishing one's own writing (S. 138) **Prime Time 6** Unit 6: Kruger National Park (S. 84) Your holiday in South Africa (S. 85) Unit 9: eSports (S. 118) Extreme sports (S. 120) Cheerleading: An extreme sport? (S. 121) **Prime Time 7** Unit 2: People with special needs (S. 30) Unit 4: Working teenagers (S. 59) Unit 5: *Into the wild* by Jon Krakauer (S. 74) Robert Falcon Scott (S. 76) Unit 7: What's a celebrity? (S. 100) The magic of Bollywood (S. 106) Unit 8: Graffiti – Vandalism or art? (S. 116) Abstract art (S. 117) **Prime Time 8** Unit 7: Spend it, spend it, spend more (S. 80) Shop 'til you drop (S. 82)
9. Consumerism	**Prime Time 5 Transition** Unit 3: Eating out (S. 38) Shopping (S. 42) **Prime Time 6** Unit 5: International outsourcing (S. 68) Unit 7: *Martin Lukes: Who Moved My BlackBerry?* by Lucy Kellaway (S. 94) **Prime Time 7** Unit 4: Working teenagers (S. 59) **Prime Time 8** Unit 3: TV and advertising (S. 32) Unit 7: Money makes the world go round (S. 78) Spend it, spend it, spend more (S. 80) Shop 'til you drop (S. 82) Marketing to children (S. 84) Shopping for happiness (S. 86) Outlet shopping (S. 88) Don't let them fool you (S. 88) Safe online shopping (S. 89)
10. Tradition and change	**Prime Time 6** Unit 1: Friendship (S. 8) Teenage pregnancies (S. 13) Unit 10: Living dolls (S. 130) **Prime Time 7** Unit 5: "Arranged marriage" by Chitra Banerjee Divakaruni (S. 68) Unit 9: The UK: Festivals and festivities (S. 133)

Topic	Vorkommen in Prime Time 5 bis 8
11. Transport and tourism	**Prime Time 5 Transition** Unit 3: The trip of a lifetime (S. 34) Eating out (S. 38) When things go wrong (S. 41) Shopping (S. 42) Unit 9: Aspects of Australia (S. 117) At the Reef in a glass-bottom boat (S. 118) **Prime Time 6** Unit 2: Video: The Notting Hill Carnival (S. 28) Unit 6: What to see and do (S. 83) The Kruger National Park (S. 84)
12. Political, historical and cultural aspects of English-speaking countries	**Prime Time 5 Transition** Unit 1: English as a world language (S. 14) Unit 9: Australia (S. 116 ff.) The stolen generations (S. 124) First time in "Oz" (S. 126) G'day from down under (S. 128) **Prime Time 6** Unit 2: Video: The Notting Hill Carnival (S. 28) Unit 6: South Africa (S. 74 ff.) She doesn't speak (S. 78) What to see and do (S. 83) The Kruger National Park (S. 84) **Prime Time 7** Unit 1: The British today (S. 6) The United Kingdom and its citizens (S. 8) Britain's search for identity (S. 9) The British character (S. 10) The legacy of the Empire (S. 12) Britain and Europe (S. 14) The hidden rules of English behaviour (S. 19) Unit 3: London – The Great Wen (S. 36) New York: The city that never sleeps (S. 38) Remote places: The American Midwest (S. 40) Remote places: The Celtic fringe (S. 42) Remote places: The US Pacific coast (S. 45) Unit 6: India (S. 82 ff.) A brief geographical and historical overview (S. 84) Mark Tully's India (S. 85) The wounds of history (S. 86) Hindu gods and goddesses (S. 87) Mahatma Gandhi – "The Great Soul" (S. 88) Controversial views (S. 89) The caste system (S. 92) India today (S. 93) Unit 9: The UK: Festivals and festivities (S. 133) **Prime Time 8** Unit 1: Ireland (S. 6 ff.) "Westering Home" by Bernard O'Donoghue (S. 8) The Pogues – Thousands are sailing (S. 8) Irish Films – Once (S. 12)
13. Art and culture	**Prime Time 5** Unit 4: The Truman Show (S. 46) The Baby Borrowers (S. 48)

Topic	Vorkommen in Prime Time 5 bis 8
13. Art and culture	Docusoaps (S. 49) A movie review (S. 51) Unit 6: Going home (S. 76) Unit 8: Producing your own music (S. 100) Protest songs (S. 103) A history of rock and pop music (S. 106) Unit 10: Talking about books (S. 128) A book review of *Holes* by Louis Sachar (S. 129) Painting pictures with words (Billy Collins: "Introduction to poetry", Flora Thomas: "Down in the greenhouse") (S. 130, S. 131) The paperless book (S. 136) The future of print media (S. 137) **Prime Time 5 Transition** Unit 5: Fake world (S. 60) Docusoaps (S. 64) A movie review (S. 66) Unit 6: Producing your own music (S. 74) Protest songs (S. 78) A history of rock and pop music (S. 81) Unit 8: Deportation at breakfast (S. 107) Unit 10: Talking about books (S. 134) A book review of *Holes* by Louis Sachar (S. 135) Painting pictures with words (Billy Collins: "Introduction to poetry", Flora Thomas: "Down in the greenhouse") (S. 136, S. 137) The paperless book (S. 142) The future of print media (S. 143) **Prime Time 6** Unit 1: *Slam* by Nick Hornby (S. 10) Unit 6: Nelson Mandela – Long walk to freedom (S. 76) "In Detention" by Christopher van Wyk (S. 77) "She doesn't speak" by Marita van der Vyver (S. 78) Unit 7: *Martin Lukes: Who Moved My BlackBerry?* by Lucy Kellaway (S. 94) Unit 8: *Looking for Alibrandi* by Melina Marchetta (S. 111) Unit 10: *Uglies* by Scott Westerfeld (S. 135) **Prime Time 7** Unit 1: "The English today" by Jeremy Paxman (S. 10) Unit 3: "New York" by Edward Field (S. 38) *What's eating Gilbert Grape?* by Peter Hedges (S. 40) *Snow falling on cedars* by David Guterson (S. 45) Unit 5: "Life is fine" by Langston Hughes (S. 67) "Arranged marriage" by Chitra Banerjee Divakaruni (S. 68) *My sister's keeper* by Jodi Picoult (S. 70) *A long way down* by Nick Hornby (S. 72) *Into the wild* by Jon Krakauer (S. 74) Unit 7: What's a celebrity? (S. 100) Paparazzi (S. 104) The magic of Bollywood (S. 106) Unit 8: Street art (S. 114) Graffiti – Vandalism or art? (S. 116) Abstract art (S. 117) Unit 9: "I think it's the architecture" by ZZ Packer (S. 130) "In my country" by Jackie King (S. 132)

Topic	Vorkommen in Prime Time 5 bis 8
13. Art and culture	The UK: Festivals and festivities (S. 133) Unit 10: The Shakespeare portrait (S. 142) What we know about William Shakespeare (S. 144) The Globe Theatre (S. 146) *Richard III* by William Shakespeare (S. 148) Ourselves in Shakespeare (S. 151) Expressions coined by Shakespeare (S. 152) Shakespeare on the silver screen (S. 153) Shakespeare's plays and money (S. 153) **Prime Time 8** Unit 1: "Westering Home" by Bernard O'Donoghue (S. 8) The Pogues – Thousands are sailing (S. 8) Irish Films – Once (S. 12) Unit 3: The Beat Generation (S. 34) Unit 7: Marketing to children (S. 84) Unit 8: The new voyeur (S. 92)
14. Media	**Prime Time 5** Unit 2: Facebook – an introduction (S. 24) Unit 4: The Truman Show (S. 46) The Baby Borrowers (S. 48) Docusoaps (S. 49) A movie review (S. 51) Unit 8: Producing your own music (S. 100) Protest songs (S. 103) A history of rock and pop music (S. 106) Unit 10: Talking about books (S. 128) A book review of *Holes* by Louis Sachar (S. 129) Painting pictures with words (Billy Collins: "Introduction to poetry", Flora Thomas: "Down in the greenhouse") (S. 130, S. 131) The paperless book (S. 136) The future of print media (S. 137) **Prime Time 5 Transition** Unit 2: Facebook – an introduction (S. 24) Unit 3: When things go wrong (S. 41) Unit 5: Fake world (S. 60) Docusoaps (S. 64) Unit 6: Producing your own music (S. 74) Protest songs (S. 78) Unit 8: Crime and suspense (S. 112) Unit 10: Talking about books (S. 134) A book review of *Holes* by Louis Sachar (S. 135) Painting pictures with words (Billy Collins: "Introduction to poetry", Flora Thomas: "Down in the greenhouse") (S. 136, S. 137) The paperless book (S. 142) The future of print media (S. 143) **Prime Time 7** Unit 7: What's a celebrity? (S. 100) Paparazzi (S. 104) The magic of Bollywood (S. 106) Unit 10: Expressions coined by Shakespeare (S. 152) Shakespeare on the silver screen (S. 153) Shakespeare's plays and money (S. 153)

Topic	Vorkommen in Prime Time 5 bis 8
14. Media	**Prime Time 8** Unit 3: TV and advertising (S. 32)
15. Communication	**Prime Time 5** Unit 1: The world speaks English (S. 9) Special English (S. 13) Unit 2: Facebook – an introduction (S. 24) Unit 7: Dignity for all? (S. 88) Tolerance and respect (S. 93) **Prime Time 5 Transition** Unit 1: English as a world language (S. 14) Unit 2: Facebook – an introduction (S. 24) Unit 5: Docusoaps (S. 64)
16. Nature and the environment	**Prime Time 5** Unit 3: *Walkabout* (S. 32) Unit 6: Going home (S. 76) The Aboriginal spiritual world (S. 77) **Prime Time 6** Unit 2: Presenting information about ethnic minorities (S. 28) Unit 3: Bag Lady (S. 36) A campaign speech (S. 37) Do food miles matter? (S. 38) Forget carbon: Check your water footprint! (S. 39) Discussing environmental issues (S. 41) Video: Mediterranean Britain (S. 42) Food miles (S. 44) Carbon footprint (S. 45) Unit 5: International outsourcing (S. 68) Unit 6: What to see and do (S. 83) Kruger National Park (S. 84) **Prime Time 8** Unit 2: Environmental footprint (S. 18) Climate change (S. 20) Video: Stuff global warming. Fly today. (S. 21) Housing 2.0 (S. 22) Eco-friends (S. 24) Green shopping? (S. 26) The future of Green America (S. 27) Climate change takes its toll on Scotland (S. 29) Unit 3: Nature or nurture (S. 36)
17. New technologies	**Prime Time 5** Unit 2: Facebook – an introduction (S. 24) Unit 10: The paperless book (S. 136) The future of print media (S. 137) **Prime Time 5 Transition** Unit 2: Facebook – an introduction (S. 24) Unit 4: Geocaching (S. 52) Unit 10: The paperless book (S. 142) The future of print media (S. 143) **Prime Time 8** Unit 2: Housing 2.0 (S. 22) Unit 7: Don't let them fool you (S. 88) Unit 8: The new voyeur (S. 92) Genetic engineering: Medicine (S. 94)

Topic	Vorkommen in Prime Time 5 bis 8
17. New technologies	Genetic modification: Food (S. 97) Nanotechnology (S. 101) Stem cells (S. 101)
18. Plans and future opportunities	**Prime Time 5** Unit 2: How I see myself (S. 16) Now that's what I call living! (S. 21) Unit 9: Work experience (S. 115) Applying for a job (S. 117) **Prime Time 5 Transition** Unit 2: How I see myself (S. 20) Now that's what I call living! (S. 26) Unit 4: Doing something sensible (S. 49) Unit 7: Work experience (S. 89) Applying for a job (S. 91) **Prime Time 8** Unit 6: A hierarchy of needs (S. 66) Volunteering (S. 68) Single and happy – It's the freemales (S. 70) The American Dream (S. 72) Choosing my religion – It's normal in the US (S. 73) What's wrong with today's youth? (S. 76)
19. Intercultural and social aspects	**Prime Time 5** Unit 1: The world speaks English (S. 9) Unit 3: Australia quiz (S. 30) *Walkabout* (S. 32) *Angela* (S. 34) First time in "Oz" (S. 38) G'day from down under (S. 40) Unit 5: Quiz: Politics in the UK (S. 62) How an MP is elected (S. 64) Different parliaments for different people (S. 65) How American democracy began (S. 69) The American Constitution and the Bill of Rights (S. 70) The American government today (S. 70) The current US President (S. 71) Unit 6: Going home (S. 76) Unit 7: The different faces of human rights (S. 86) Values as the basis of human rights (S. 87) Dignity for all? (S. 88) Tolerance and respect (S. 93) Heroes: The power of pictures (S. 95) Internet project: "The mean girl" (S. 95) **Prime Time 5 Transition** Unit 9: Australia quiz (S. 116) *Walkabout* (S. 122) *Angela* (S. 119) First time in "Oz" (S. 126) G'day from down under (S. 128) The stolen generations (S. 124) **Prime Time 6** Unit 2: Caribbean London (S. 20) Video: Caribbeans in London (S. 21) Hope of escape lost in translation (S. 24) Interview with Mary Douglas (S. 26)

Topic	Vorkommen in Prime Time 5 bis 8
19. Intercultural and social aspects	Presenting information about ethnic minorities (S. 28) Video: The Notting Hill Carnival (S. 28) Looking at food in the UK (S. 30) Unit 5: Globalisation: Not new at all … (S. 62) The British Empire (S. 64) The Americanisation of the world? (S. 70) Unit 6: What to see and do (S. 83) Unit 8: "I have a dream" by Martin Luther King, Jr. (S. 104) A speech by Lenny Henry (S. 115) Unit 9: Cheerleading: An extreme sport? (S. 121) **Prime Time 7** Unit 1: The United Kingdom and its citizens (S. 8) Britain's search for an identity (S. 9) The legacy of the Empire (S. 12) The Commonwealth of Nations (S. 13) Britain's future tied to Europe (S. 14) The hidden rules of English behaviour (S. 19) Unit 3: Regional identities (London, New York, Celtic Fringe, US Pacific Coast) (S. 34 ff.) Unit 6: India (S. 82 ff.) Unit 9: The psychology of stereotypes (S. 127) Can we improve on affirmative action? (S. 128) "I think it's the architecture" by ZZ Packer (S. 130) Video: American immigration: Failure to stem immigration tide (S. 131) "In my country" by Jackie King (S. 132) Lord Morris of Handsworth (S. 132) The UK: Festivals and festivities (S. 133) British Muslims (S. 134) Three generations, two cultures (S. 136) Reflections of a former British Muslim extremist (S. 139) A sense of community (S. 139) **Prime Time 8** Unit 1: Ireland (S. 6 ff.) Unit 4: Canada: Attentive acupuncturist (S. 44) How to immigrate to Canada (S. 45) United States: An immigrant's long journey (S. 46) UK: Immigration – Two opposing views (S. 50) Canada: New pioneers (S. 52) Unit 6: The American Dream (S. 72) Hero – Tariq Jahan (S. 75)
20. Growing up	**Prime Time 5** Unit 2: How I see myself (S. 20) "Let no one steal your dreams" by Paul Cookson (S. 20) Unit 8: Protest songs (S. 103) Unit 10: Don't judge a book by its cover (S. 126) **Prime Time 5 Transition** Unit 4: Doing something sensible (S. 49) Unit 5: Docusoaps (S. 64) Unit 7: Work experience (S. 89) Unit 8: Juvenile crime (S. 102) Unit 9: *Angela* (S. 119) **Prime Time 6** Unit 1: Friendship (S. 8)

Topic	Vorkommen in Prime Time 5 bis 8
20. Growing up	Teenage pregnancies (S. 13)
	Unit 6: Nelson Mandela – Long walk to freedom (S. 76)
	"In Detention" by Christopher van Wyk (S. 77)
	"She doesn't speak" by Marita van der Vyver (S. 78)
	Unit 7: A quiz: How motivated are you? (S. 88)
	Martin Lukes: Who Moved My BlackBerry? by Lucy Kellaway (S. 94)
	Unit 10: Living dolls (S. 130)
	Prime Time 7
	Unit 2: You are what you eat (S. 22)
	People with special needs (S. 30)
	Unit 3: *What's eating Gilbert Grape?* by Peter Hedges (S. 40)
	Unit 4: First love (S. 52)
	Entering adulthood (S. 56)
	Britain's lost talent (S. 58)
	Working teenagers (S. 59)
	Unit 5: "Arranged marriage" by Chitra Banerjee Divakaruni (S. 68)
	My sister's keeper by Jodi Picoult (S. 70)
	Saving his sister's life (S. 71)
	A long way down by Nick Hornby (S. 72)
	Into the wild by Jon Krakauer (S. 74)
	Robert Falcon Scott (S. 76)
	Unit 9: "I think it's the architecture" by ZZ Packer (S. 130)
	"In my country" by Jackie King (S. 132)
	Prime Time 8
	Unit 2: Eco-friends (S. 24)
	Unit 3: S/HE (S. 30)
	Women in the 1950s (S. 34)
	Transsexuality (S. 41)
	Unit 5: Seeds of peace (S. 58)
	Unit 6: A hierarchy of needs (S. 66)
	Volunteering (S. 68)
	Single and happy – It's the freemales (S. 70)
	The American Dream (S. 72)
	Choosing my religion – It's normal in the US (S. 73)
	A glimpse at Hazel's life (S. 74)
	Hero – Tariq Jahan (S. 75)
	What's wrong with today's youth? (S. 76)
	Unit 7: Marketing to children (S. 84)
21. Politics and public institutions	**Prime Time 5**
	Unit 5: Quiz: Politics in the UK (S. 62)
	How an MP is elected (S. 64)
	Different parliaments for different people (S. 65)
	How American democracy began (S. 69)
	The American Constitution and the Bill of Rights (S. 70)
	The American government today (S. 70)
	The current US President (S. 71)
	Prime Time 8
	Unit 1: The Troubles (S. 9)
	Unit 5: International peacekeeping (S. 55)
	The United Nations at work (S. 56)
	Seeds of peace (S. 58)
	Superpowers? (S. 60)
	NGOs at work in China (S. 64)

Topic	Vorkommen in Prime Time 5 bis 8
22. Globalisation	**Prime Time 5 Transition** Unit 1: Just another pizza order in Manhattan (S. 10) English as a world language (S. 14) **Prime Time 6** Unit 5: Globalisation: Not new at all … (S. 62) The three eras of globalisation (S. 63) The British Empire (S. 64) International outsourcing (S. 68) The Americanisation of the world? (S. 70) The global village (S. 72) Unit 7: *Martin Lukes: Who Moved My BlackBerry?* by Lucy Kellaway (S. 94) **Prime Time 7** Unit 4: Working teenagers (S. 59) Unit 5: Stress management (S. 77) Coping with stress (S. 78) Exam stress (S. 81) **Prime Time 8** Unit 3: Advertising strategies (S. 33) Unit 7: Spend it, spend it, spend more (S. 80) Shop 'til you drop (S. 82) Marketing to children (S. 84)
23. Social groups and minorities	**Prime Time 5 Transition** Unit 4: Doing something sensible (S. 49) Unit 6: Protest songs (S. 78) Unit 8: Juvenile crime (S. 102) Deportation at breakfast (S. 107) Unit 9: *Angela* (S. 119) The stolen generations (S. 124) **Prime Time 7** Unit 2: People with special needs (S. 30) Unit 4: Entering adulthood (S. 56) Britain's lost talent (S. 58) Working teenagers (S. 59) Unit 9: The US: Racial (in)equality – the legal situation (S. 128) The US: Racial (in)equality – in real life (S. 130) British Muslims (S. 134) The Mattani family: Three generations, two cultures (S. 136) **Prime Time 8** Unit 3: S/HE (S. 30) Women in the 1950s (S. 34) Transsexuality (S. 41)
24. Rules, regulations and legal matters	**Prime Time 5 Transition** Unit 3: When things go wrong (S. 41) Unit 8: Juvenile crime (S. 102) Crime and suspense (S. 112) **Prime Time 7** Unit 4: PM speaks out against youth knife crime (S. 62) The PAYP scheme (S. 64) Unit 8: Graffiti – Vandalism or art? (S. 116) Abstract art (S. 117) **Prime Time 8** Unit 6: Personal freedom (S. 70) Single and happy: It's the freemales (S. 70)

Topics 1–24 Key

Topic 4 Nutrition, health and welfare (Key)

3 How to start a sentence

I am not in a position to comment on … .
I am not in a position to judge … .
I don't think that … .
My feeling is that … .
I don't want to comment on … .
Well, actually, … .
I find it hard to … .
I personally … .
I really think that … .
I would rather not comment on … .
I've honestly never thought about … .
If you ask me, … .
In my opinion, … .
It depends on what you mean by … .
It is hard to say … .
It's really quite simple … .
Look at it this way … .

Topic 10 Tradition and change (Key)

1 Talking about old and new

a) **Old:** conservative, conventional, dated, old-fashioned, old-school , old-style, out-dated, out-of-date, traditional, unfashionable
New: brand-new, contemporary, current, fashionable, innovative, latest, modern, recent, state-of-the-art, trendy, up-to-date
b) **Synonyms of destruction:** to demolish, to destroy, to raze to the ground, to tear down
Synonyms of reconstruction: to keep, to modernise, to preserve, to rebuild, to reconstruct, to refurbish, to renovate, to repair,

Topic 14 Media (Key)

3 Vocabulary revision: Media

1. book, **2.** website, **3.** newspaper, **4.** radio, **5.** television

Topic 18 Plans and future opportunities (Key)

1 Expressing certainty

a) **Beispielantwort**
1. D, **2.** H, **3.** I, **4.** L, **5.** J, **6.** A, **7.** K, **8.** E, **9.** B, **10.** G, **11.** F, **12.** C

Topic 20 Growing up (Key)

1 Reacting to statements: Expressing doubt

a) **Beispielantwort**
1. G, **2.** I, **3.** D, **4.** F, **5.** C, **6.** A, **7.** E, **8.** J, **9.** B, **10.** H

Topic 24 Rules, regulations and legal matters (Key)

2 Concluding

Beispielantwort
1. D, **2.** H, **3.** K, **4.** F, **5.** C, **6.** M, **7.** I, **8.** J, **9.** A, **10.** L, **11.** N, **12.** B, **13.** G, **14.** E